Crossing the Heads

Also by John Egan and published by Ginninderra Press

Lines Continue Forever
The Long Way Home
Reworkings (Pocket Poets)
Reworkings 2 (Pocket Poets)
Reworkings 3 (Pocket Poets)
Reworkings 4 (Pocket Poets)
Reworkings 5 (Pocket Poets)
Sydney Central (Pocket Poets)
Play It Louder (Pocket Poets)
Putting to Sea (Pocket Poets)
A Safe Harbour

John Egan

Crossing the Heads

Acknowledgements

Some of the poems in this collection first appeared in
*Beyond the Rainbow, Positive Words, The Mozzie, Ripples, Polestar,
Five Bells, The Write Angle, Poetry Matters, Pendulum, WritingRAW.com,
The Valley Micropress, Tamba, FreeXpresion, The Senior*
and in the anthology *Northern Lights*.

'The Pain from the Past' – 1st Prize, The Writers' Friend
Competition 2009

Crossing the Heads
ISBN 978 1 76041 375 0
Copyright © text John Egan 2017
Author photo: Peter Egan
Front cover photo: Sea N Head set cliffs vertical © Taras Vyshnya

First published 2017 by
GINNINDERRA PRESS
PO Box 3461 Port Adelaide 5015 Australia
www.ginninderrapress.com.au

Contents

Crossing the Heads	11
The Ferry	13
Coal Ships at Newcastle	14
A Cormorant	15
Megalong	16
Angels in Sydney	17
Clumsy Angels	18
Already	19
A Good Student	20
Tears	23
Light Rain, November	24
Hydrangeas	25
Don't Go There	26
Driving South	27
Twenty-four Hours	29
Steps to There	30
Iron Cove	31
Cambewarra Winery	32
St Stephen's Churchyard, Newtown	33
Villanelle of the New Day	35
Morning Arrivals	36
Cathay Pacific	37
Approaching Home	38
Landing from the north	39
Waiting	40
Don't Touch	41
Inner Child	42
Three Men	44
Walking Through Paddington	46
King's Cross, Victoria Street	47
Ashfield Afternoon	49

Shuffling	50
Glenfield Station	51
Barangaroo	53
An Old Mohawk	54
The Energy of Spring	57
Spring	58
Ordeal	59
Nothing Like My life	60
Fromelles	62
A War Memorial	63
Ghosts and Dreams	65
Opening Night	66
6 a.m. Fog, Sydney, Early Winter	68
On the Death of Slobodan Milosevic	70
The Father of Ashes	72
Berry Mountain Road	73
'Home'	74
Finger Wharf	77
Reservoir Street, Surry Hills	78
Now	80
The Horse and the Cattle Dog	81
Toby	83
Late Afternoon, Camperdown Park	85
A Mad Moon	86
It	87
On the Hawkesbury	88
A River, Anywhere	89
Old Paris	90
Sullivan's Cove, Midnight	91
No New Start	93
White	94
The Mist	95
Widow	96

Untitled	97
The Cathedral	98
UTS Tower, Broadway	99
Central Park, Broadway	100
Reflections	101
New Tickets	102
Perfection	104
J.M.W. Turner: *The Fighting Temeraire, 1838*	105
Irene, Dance	107
Black Curtains	108
The Well	109
Back Veranda	110
It's a Right	111
Sonnet 127 Again	112
Sharrukina Reads 'The Outcast'	113
After the Explosion	114
Just Stepping Out	115
At Night	116
From the Bistro	117
The Pain From the Past is Always Present	118
Smile	119
Potential	120
Birdsong	121
Thunderclouds	122
Thunderstorm	123
Vibrant	124
Like Losing Skin	125
Christmas 2014	126
A Dress of Words	127
Night Ferry to Abbotsford	128
The River and the City	129

In memory of my father Maurice (Morrie) Egan
(1923–2007),
who first taught me to read
and aroused my interest in literature.

'…the hovering sky and the hydrofoil and a lick of the sea
till you'd swear it was Venice and, hell, here it's only Sydney…'

John Couper, 'Crossing the Bridge'

Crossing the Heads

No swell through the heads tonight,
the harbour flat as stale champagne,
memory leaving a sunlit beach.

The *Queenscliff* churns to the south of Manly,
scissors a course, the black abyss,
the bulk of George's Head, starboard no stars,
not a light among the bush and cliff.
Stand on the point of the bow, lean forward,
watch the ship's forefoot pressing down
as if it asks a question, just to smash
the answer into chaos in its wake.

A geometry of ripples spreads a face
across the water, swirls and eddies
to a texture that carpets the blackness
into ridges. The wind builds sand tracks
in a pattern that the ship,
like a tractor, pushes into furrows.

Beat upharbour, beacons green and red,
bend and twist the channel, align
the starlight and the neon city.
Irregular the intervals between,
passing one, the next slides into view,
like the seasons or the numbered calendar
of days. What lies below the surface? Faces
looking down, faces peering back.

We are here, turning south of the green
at fourteen knots, north of bays and darkness,
the track of navigation lights, the rolling pulse
of diesels driving to the red.
What highway this? Why embarked
a lonely voyage into night? Why this ship,
headlands and harbour light?

Our course is set by chart and bearing,
the foot of wilderness, this far crossing,
the wide Pacific gapes away to the world
and we are sliding towards a neat,
new berth, light-swept wharves, silent,
welcome as a warm hotel, but
what new port and what strange night?

The Ferry

Tonight
the wind scatters stars
among the ghost gums
and the light years.

The Milky Way's a river.

The wide universe
engraved with lights
for navigation,
the channels and the beacons.

Stars in torrents
and tributaries in surge.
Old suns swing
their probes and light shafts,

lighthouse galaxies,
the headland stars
shimmer and sweep
in the waves.

Time is a ferry
that glides downstream,
the farthest reaches,
the surest flow.

The river and the stars
that steer the years,
highways to the tides
of the gathering sea.

Coal Ships at Newcastle

From Throsby Basin to Pirate Point,
past Nobby's Head, their spawning grounds the sea,
bulk ships lumber in. Empty, obese,
the monsters roll beside the city, red
on bulwark hulls, colliers and black ships
breakwater-sheer rise from the arching sea.
They swing to the Hunter's northbound channel
like bastions flanked by tugs, tall as castles
walking in the street, they drum and shudder
slowly by to Kooragang to gorge on coal.

Gale-lashed, *Pasher Bulker*, riding high –
ballast emptied hours too soon – too light
to steam for the open sea, her single screw
churned to grip and headway lost, wind-wrecked, wallowed
in the thin, fast water, surge tides
and wind-whipped swells. Force eight south-easterlies,
express-train speeds, dragged her anchors landwards,
scraped the reef and rammed the boiling surf,
struck like flotsam, piled-up, fast aground,
suburban Nobby's Beach.

Rain and sleet, tides and wind and swell –
mariners beware a low, ship-breaking coast,
rocks and sand. When air pressure falls to grim
steam to sea, outrun the storm; keep hard ballast
in your tanks, sea miles wide across your bows.
Your forbears and musclemen, watchful sailors –
Flinders, Bass and Cook, heroes of sail, lived
the sea's heartbeat, breathed its moods, not diesel
pumps and dials, smelt the wind's change, always kept
clear water deep below their keels.

A Cormorant

A silhouette
against the blue,
black and willowy,
flies wide circuits
around the bay,
claws lowered
skimming the waves,
combs the surface
like radar

and is gone, diving,
then resurfaces
like a shadow,

is gone again
for minutes
and is there
suddenly
against the sun,

black
like a shard of night
as the sky sparkles
in the afternoon,
which is also gone
too soon.

Megalong

There's a blackbird on a high branch,
all the valley watches below.

Bare trees here, an airscape of sky,
laments of fall, the hollow breath
of fat-cushioned clouds, safe, afloat,
harnessed above the shallow wind.

Faraway, slopes swept with blue gums
flow down from a ragged skyline,
shadows sketched across the valley,
yellow cliffs worn by the air's long rubbing
and the relentless weight of water.

This landscape seems eternal now
falls in slow and stately rhythms,
drawn within the blackbird's eye.

Angels in Sydney

A painting by Nadine Sawyer

Harlequins in colour,
acrobats in curve and grace,
the glamour of their kisses
in the jewelled air.

Rainbows spun from gossamer,
sprites that dance in carnival,
power and spirit, abstract, here,
entirely the ephemeral,

slip between our sight, our dreams
in comedy, in joy and flight.
Clowns sweep down from heaven still
radiant from being there.

Clumsy Angels

The sad beauty of this awkward flight,
clumsy angels dump their vapour trails
across the numinous moment, a void
between their actions and desire, altars
of stars in congregation, the fulcrum
point of time poised between now and turning,
when potential grows to power
or collapses into grief, the blue-cotton sky
and butter-smooth sun or the slow death
of planets. Fallible angels, limping spirits,
smear the moment, the flower that doesn't
bloom, the dream that never wakes, ugly sprites
from black suns waste their days, they wait
outside the rusting gates of Eden, forever bolted.

Already

If you want to look as if
you've just staggered into town
after wandering crazed in the desert,
eyes glazed by the sun,
cheeks gouged by hunger,
tongue swollen black
in the hollow of your mouth,
hallucinations shimmering
of weird, cold water,
as you collapse incoherent
in the screeching air,
the first shade you've seen
since the shrill, demon-clawing night…

then just wait, let life
take its course. It will…already
the sun's blazing like a drill,
the dams are low and falling. There are
sand dunes knocking against the fence…

A Good Student

At thirteen or fourteen
was a good student,
except at physical education,
couldn't see the point of sport,
slightly uncoordinated,
not that you'd notice
except at sport.
Years later, an adult, I read
pre-term babies often are
and I was very premature,
lucky to have lived.
I didn't know that then.

Sitting in class, our English teacher
late, reading the class novel –
David Copperfield, I think –
engrossed, lost to the world,
in another, earlier world,
then a roaring in my ears:
GET ON YER FEET!
GET ON YER FEET!
The PE teacher,
yelling at me –
he'd slipped in quietly,
nattered to his favourites,
the good sportsmen, down the front,
then expected our attention
without bothering
to call us together –
years later I knew, execrable
teaching technique – always
mark the point the lesson begins,
call the class together, get all
their attention, then start.
I know, forty years a teacher!

GET ON YER FEET!
WHAT SPORT DO YOU PLAY, SON!
Stunned, I stammered, 'Tennis'.
TENNIS WHAT? All I could think of:
Tennis. TENNIS SIR!
What had I done? Read a book,
was a good student, I thought.

He yelled abuse, release of spite,
ridicule, humiliation, in front of the class,
said, 'If you play tennis, son,
there's something wrong between your legs!
A game for girls! Manly boys play rugby'
is all I remember now.

Angry he'd got an extra, last-minute,
lost his free period, took it out on me.
I was thirteen or fourteen, read books,
wore glasses, played tennis,
hated sport, hated him –
he couldn't teach me a bloody thing,
didn't even try, just loved the good sportsmen,
talked to them, liked to
touch them in the gym –
something wrong between MY legs –
even then I didn't think so.

That was fifty years ago,
he's dead now.
Good thing!

Tears

There are tears in all things,
dark messengers among the stones
and fear edged in the whispers of birds,
in syllables that curve
into slow doom that falls like rain.
There's poison in the bloodstream,
in the massed storm troops, of ideas
and our needs in electric love.

Despite anger and the wheels of time,
we live in the core,
in flurries of delight,
pinpricks of touch,
in songs delicate as an eyelash
or butterflies of tarnished bronze.

Light Rain, November

The city softened by showers and mist,
hard edges rounded into grey and light,
the bridge arched into cloud and pearls flicker
on the soft harbour, merging into sky.

The fountain sprays particles of silver
into a brimming bowl – they slide like teardrops
down rotund sides into an earth that's moist
with connection, damp with air, damp

with the day breathing out like dew.
Everywhere the blaze of jacarandas
like blue sunburst muted under water,

flowerburst filtered by moisture, diffused
in lawn carpets, purple raincoats, surreal
among grey and olive-green and tearfulness.

Hydrangeas

Hydrangeas open their leaves,
hands held in prayer, seeking
blessings and forgiveness. The imminent
rain splatters nervously, distant thunder,
the edge of the approaching storm.

But their flowers tighten
into balls, huddle defensively
with an intransigence that repels rain,
as if protecting themselves from hurt
and looking inwards mutter reject, reject,

gather impervious in their blinded blue
to the clean droplets, the grey clouds.
Sedate in their beauty, they scorn the world,
its energy and change, contemplate only
pleasure and youth, comfort, themselves.

Don't Go There

There's no highway when looking for the past,
road signs and traffic glowing nonetheless.
Fake shamans block the path, glibly confess
errors in witchcraft, gross defects that blast
even the present – still spellbound, unmasked
by the glamour of fashion and fame, the mess
that spoils the evening-gown sheen of women dressed
as angels of the road, mere actors cast
in a scene of freeways you can't forget.
No, you'll never go back, there's no road there.
Walk the streets, examine facades and yet
houses empty of dreams. Old windows stare
and footpaths entice you somewhere else – let
thin veneers just moulder, useless and bare.

Driving South

There's satisfaction and a thrill
in backing out the car,
locking down the garage door
and your ETA is two hour's south,
the road that ribbons on the coast,

as if your safety belt's fastened,
tray and seat-back snapped to upright,
the runway charges into blurred and eagle-clawed
your Boeing slips the ground, rotates upwards,
flattens out its gravity and surges
across the bay – four big turbofans
that lift their jet stream and soar towards the coast.

In fact, you slide to 'drive', throttle and rev,
manipulate the flow and veer of traffic.
Directions straddle your wheel-lock tyres,
hands caress to steer, fingers trace
contours on maps, the dimensions
of highways like flight paths to the sky.

Flutter into winglock like a hawk.
Feathers hiss to grip the gridlines,
eyes shudder and switch, your airstream
wing tips navigate the airwaves homewards
to the sun. The blacktop's rolling by,
macadam slides between your heels,
velocities of steel and space perform
a syncopated melody of miles.
Your wingspan beats in tracks across the stars,
in rising thermals and the latitude
of winds that weave your flight path here.

The distant rhythm of a broken range
and the ridge that parallels your flight
converge like meridians on a globe
and twist through hills at Broughton Mill
where idling creeks and stone-crossed rivers flow.
The earthbound paddocks and the calm of trees.
The highway brings this driver home.
Here is the raptor home from the sky,
the traveller in from the sea.

Twenty-four Hours

The foggy highway shimmers
into burnished morning.
The day's a mirror and the lake
reflects nothing but the creek, pleated
in a slurry of spray and whispers,
the shrapnelled droplets
that a rusting gutter weeps
into a spangle of tears.

The crumpled river runs and the highways
grieve for a corner of life.
Wind-shrugging like a discarded page,
the afternoons are tarnished
by the drift of stream and sunlight
towards another ordinary midnight.

Steps to There

Velocity beats and minutes burn
into highways and distance, siren skies,
the future like songs to the moon

and the complex arithmetic of now.
Here is time passing, beams of light
and the quick poetry of soon.

Sleeping cars and night expresses.
Trains depart this track for there,

tomorrow, via here tonight and now,
is all we know of motion and each hour.

Iron Cove

Walk the path beside the bay,
the mist rising, the shadow of a boat
passing with throbs across the quiet water
and the morning beginning to open
into sunlight and warmth.

The path winds through groves of trees.
The launch continues its straight course
from point to point, while I twist between parks,
bushes and fences, taking the longer track.

I watch the boat disappear around the headland.
Its silver wake shimmers, vanishes,
as the morning sun smoothes the day with its vision
of neatness, order, predictability.

On the distant side of the cove, stacked on
the uncertain shore, red suburban roofs,
like a jigsaw puzzle, started but not complete,
and the main road stressed with traffic,

fluid monotony, featureless and flat.
Joggers and walkers follow routine paths
and cross only on the zebra crossings.
From the jumble there to trees and shade here

before the sun begins to prise apart
the morning into heat and noise and glare.

Cambewarra Winery

for Louise Cole

A late afternoon pinpoints leaves
on every vine. They curl and cling
along the wire, climb and claw
towards the ridge, the hump and spine

of Cambewarra, perspectives framed
between the sunlight and the lake.
Shadows from a monolith
like colours in a glass. The mountain's vineyard,

layers of alluvium and silt,
Shoalhaven's floodplain, river flats.
The grapes of sunslope stark on the vines
Under the mountain, the rich, red wine.

St Stephen's Churchyard, Newtown

I stand in a destruction of gravestones.
Locked behind walls, memorials and tombs
are forfeit to the voracious growth of grass,
the overburden of trees and branches,
the wind, the heat, the rain.
The oldest inscriptions are now unreadable.
Many are fallen, most cracked or shattered,
some by the hands of men. An angel stands
eroded into shapeless rock.
Here too the jungle thrives.

I think of young men, convicted
in a foreign court, both locked
in the Alcatraz of no return, their lives
forfeit to the state, who will be shot
for crimes committed by their former selves.
The stench of heat, jungle-thick humidity,
and there the earth will absorb their bodies
and they, fallen in a hail of bullets,
will become the earth. Even their gravestones
will not survive the mad rush to growth.

St Stephen's Church, tower and spire,
for all its reaching to the sky and heaven,
remains a ground based form, still hugs the earth
like a gigantic, fallen cross.
It too marks an execution, a prophet
who preached love, forgiveness of sin, who lived
to save criminals like those men,
when society preferred them dead.
The firing squad, the noose, the poison gas
are the spawn of the Roman cross
that survives in the floor plan of this church.

Memorial to a more positive age,
its buttresses and plate tracery,
gables, pinnacles of stone, might impress
as symbols of certainty and power
until you see the walls themselves
shielded by a sprawl of gravel
to keep the vegetation out.

All returns to the earth, the living, as well,
all our memorials to the dead. The church
becomes the earth. All is Gaia, goddess
of life and growth, who is the earth, who holds
all things in her great cycles of creation
and death, in her terrible hands like a mother.

Villanelle of the New Day

Already darkness hums to morning
like a curtain rising on a play,
the day's conflicts gathering.

The prologue offers little warning
as the stars roll themselves away.
As the darkness hums to morning

comes the new foreboding
woven in the fabric of the day,
the hours of conflict gathering.

Spotlights illuminate the swarming
of actors who jostle for their say
as the darkness hums to morning

and the lonely traffic building
towards its climax black midday,
all the hours of conflict gathering

and the sun already surging
in this drama clothed as play.
Already darkness hums to morning
and the day's conflict gathering.

Morning Arrivals

You were coming home
from the far side of the continent
after weeks away,
the lonely desert.

That morning I stood
beside my bedroom window, watched
the distant planes in single file
drop across the rooftops, glide lower
on their flight path down towards
Kingsford Smith, disappear
behind the trees, the slight buzz
of their engines lingering for moments
then fading into the past.

I wondered, were you on one of those,

your Boeing vectored, as most are,
to the north to join the traffic
descending the morning glide path home.

When I spoke to you later I learned
you'd arrived late the previous day
and that morning you were fast asleep,
already safe in your own bed.
I felt somehow betrayed
as if you'd drifted past me in the night.

The planes descend every morning
in ordered lines across my window
and I think of you
somewhere else.

Cathay Pacific

Driving to work,
tedious, grimy suburbs,
the Inner West
and the morning traffic.

Jetburst looming from the sky…

giant, hovering stately there,
a fantasy of landing-gear and white,
spinning metropolis of air.

Palaces and towers, the planets
and the turbines of the floating north,
wing tips traced in streamers,
jet trails woven into condensation.

Pennants and cloudstreaks flutter through the mist,
vapour trails of silk, the jet stream, spindrift
flagship of the dawn, seconds out
from touchdown on its late, final

straight-line cascade into morning here.
Dull suburbs in the rain and the vast
visitors of grace that hang
like monuments across the world.

Approaching Home

Three more hours
and somewhere south of Darwin
a familiar sun rises
above the curved horizon,
the window shutters opening
onto a new morning.

Here there are white clouds below us
and blue sky as there always is
at forty thousand feet above the desert
and the old, brown continent
sweeping away beneath our wings,

the plane's computers set unerringly
for the gentle, northern flight path down
over jigsaw suburbs to Kingsford Smith,
my home just there, off to starboard,
as the ship glides on, glides in –
only three more hours cramped
in the blue immensity of somewhere.

Landing from the north

the count of air miles left to fly
clicks to lower,
airspeed drops,
the clouds that were purring cats
on carpets
miles below
now clutch and claw
our windows,
then suddenly give up.

The suburbs just erupt.
Maps flower with dimensions,
mosaics of rooftops,
blocks of buildings,
mats and quilts of parks and grass.
Roads and railways
rush to ribbons
and waterways –
rivers, harbour, bays –
fly upwards into blue.

The world expands
and rises
into real.

Waiting

Railway stations
and airports.

Black locomotives
and the red rakes of carriages.
Sleeping cars and mail.
White steam and mist.
Smoke drifts through the air.

Jet planes nose
against the glass.
Backpacks and boarding passes.
Departure lounges.
A boarding call
that must come soon.
The smell of kerosene.

Fantasies and doubts.
This is not the journey
nor the destination.

Desires and dreams
are still
frozen in waiting.

Don't Touch

Push away the bullying day,
embrace the ease of night,
turn over, shut your eyes, daydream, doze.
Keep the venetians closed,
the solid curtains drawn
against the morning's light.

Don't touch your glasses,
placed the night before carefully
next to the lamp, beside you,
on the bedside table. Leave them there.
Let the world stay unclear,
ill-defined, beyond the grasp of eyes,
the mind's pedantic analysis.

It's six in the morning. Who wants
the day's multitude of details
staring at you, roll calls
of commitments, regiments of responsibility
in rank and file, random facts
and chores in queues, anxious for answers now.

When the eyes can't focus
the world's abstract, consistent, flat,
everything in order is disorder
and there's no such thing as mess.

Inner Child

There is a child who's laughing.
There is a child who sees a joke
in the serious and grim,

who weaves a laughter curtain
between himself and other things,
who's moved by the horror he sees

but like a plump, round doll,
knocked senseless to the ground,
always rights himself again

as if vile, unspeakable acts
are only scenes in the drama
and he's the actor who plays his role

but is not involved.
There is a child who dances
through the massacre, who sings

as the city burns, who smiles
at the absurd in the heart of war.

There is a man who studies the world,
who reads of brutality and death,
is serious, severe and never smiles

who summarises the point of all gross
complexity in the dry words of law,
and reduces the heart's complications

to the simple, clear-cut and rational
and is respected and is rewarded
when he frowns and utters clichés.

He's master of the trite, criticises
disapproves and announces that he feels
every atrocity as if

it's inflicted on himself.
There is a man who always has
an opinion about everything

but he never dances or sings.
There is a child inside this man.
The man's the mask the child wears

that the world sees and steps aside,
while the child is laughing
and keeps on singing and keeps dancing.

Three Men

Fair hair, swept back and up.
A handsome face, strong, severe features.
A man in his late twenties,
dressed formally, a patterned tie
and white collar, for this
significant occasion, posed
in the photographer's studio,
his strength and youth presented in sepia,
his clear eyes looking forward
to a future he never had.
Gassed on the Western Front, then
hard, physical labour
as a locomotive fireman, dead
of wounds and exhaustion at thirty-two.

Black, severe, romantic hair, greying,
slightly receding, older but still handsome,
face a little wrinkled, this man's
an executive, striped tie
and business suit. He holds a telephone
to his ear as if in conference
but the same clear, blue eyes,
the same direct stare, posed
at his desk for the camera
as if inviting comment, conversation.
Depression kid, five years in the air force,
a successful career in printing,
a productive life, died of age
and emphysema at eighty-four.

Fair hair, lots of it, swept up
and across, but this man wears glasses,
has a moustache and looks away
from the camera into the distance,
His blue eyes are somehow not here,
not engaged, they ponder something else,
somewhere else, over there…
A posed photo but surreal,
somehow strange.
A striped tie yes, but over his jacket
a black academic gown, teacher,
actor, poet, dreamer…

These men have the same high foreheads,
the same nose, ears and pointed chins
but each confronts the camera differently,
display dissimilar attitudes to now,
their different times,
different lives
and yet there's something fundamental,
something there.

All about the same age,
three generations of men,
the same family,
my grandfather, my father, me.

Walking Through Paddington

An autumn sky, canopies of trees, leaves
scattered on the pavement like bones
but red and gold fading against grey asphalt,
damp mulch, slippery beneath my feet.

The streets push downhill, walls of houses locked
in unison, vaults and pillars in caves,
railings and gates that guide my footsteps
towards a distant city, mirage in the sky.

It floats above a possible horizon,
and might be rattling closer with each step
towards this tunnel's mouth, the safe escape.
Vacant verandas and footpaths ripped apart,

torn by subterranean claws,
roots tangled in the maze I'm toiling through,
armed only with the names of streets, turnings
to left or right, scribbled on notepaper,

crumpled in my pocket, my only chart,
the fragile thread I follow to escape
the urban Minotaur, my reason to walk, who
might still lumber behind me, not dead yet.

King's Cross, Victoria Street

A clear, blue sky and the plane trees
arch along the street, the ribs
of a green cathedral, the long nave
that guides the eye towards a high altar,

But there is no altar, only the sky,
only bays and columns of apartment buildings
and the tall terraces of a previous age,
the houses of the rich who lived here
above the slums, the wharves and the hovels
down the short walk, the narrow steps below the ridge.

Walk this street again, sit for coffee,
watch backpackers hurry from their hostels,
the shrill laughter of the girls, the waiters
trendy and polite who move with the harmony
and style of arrondissements on the Seine, as if
in certainty of having been always here.

Walk this street again, absorb its calm,
its elegance, the cosmopolitan and chic,
as if the age of gaslight and hansom cabs
survives here as a kind of nostalgia,
glamour that lingers above the drone of traffic.
The high gothic of the nineteenth century
hovers over the shrieking twenty-first.

A cathedral builds here above the gaudy
restrained, ageless, the synchronicity
of a more steadfast world, the permanence
of rows of shade trees, the arched branches
of the green world that guards the street
and spreads its pillars and its roots
like foundations in the certainty of here.

Ashfield Afternoon

Mellow and cool the surfaces,
a child's bright alphabet
in all the colours of parked cars,
neatly arranged in rows.

The orange/red of terracotta –
roof-tiles spotlit, squared and patterned
by the setting sun. Window frames
in verdant green, luxuriant as grass

and the grooves of brickwork lozenges,
the mortared edge of detail, tinged
with the eye of the low-rayed sun,
rich and soft and creamy deep.

The building's brown and textured wall
becomes a work of surreal art
displayed behind the blocks of cars,
eggshell blue, the brittle and unbroken sky.

Second storey pillars push their shadows
onto balconies, grey and concrete walls
of monastery and masonry, distance
softened in the ramparts of romanesque.

The basilica's evening cadence and chant
hovers into Charlotte Street. Afternoons
of gentle light, at just this hour,
just this place, breathe and glow.

Shuffling

This silver, rolling tube, this long chamber
on its roadbed, slim parallels of steel
and the new world's riding backwards
into the past and roads that start
so near their end, houses that dart
back to their own departure points
and the history of all those minutes
in what they were and where and when
but are no longer here.

The future's fading now, the past
keeps coming forward and City Rail's
no more than this, our morning's time machine,
less than the red-shift galaxies flying apart,
more, the shuffling on of rails and signals.
The train's streamlined here, time away and out,
rides the rails towards our newest past.
The window. See how the future doesn't last.

Glenfield Station

A station's where you make decisions.
Thirty minutes for the train home,
home by a different line – East Hills
to the airport, then the familiar world
at Central. A small adventure, riding
an unknown train on a different track.
But in that time, three trains express to home,
the faster route I've always taken.

Walk to the end of the platform,
the mainline, four tracks south,
a vision of parallels sliding
into time, but the view displaced
by flyover and bridge, the new line
smoothing its way south-west to Leppington,
a place I've been to once and know
I needn't go today.

In the everyday partings
of roads and ways, decisions loom, railways
continue on to unfamiliar places.
Make a multitude of small decisions,
the consequences may be vast
or never known for years,
sometimes you just never know.
A universe of alternatives rejected.
What might have happened if…?

I choose the less familiar train
and watch a different world roll by,
more trees and greenery, newer suburbs
but the end of the journey's
underground and the stations all the same.
The road not taken is the one I took
and the train I chose has made perhaps
a difference, but I think not much.
The repercussions I doubt will be severe.

Barangaroo

Hundreds of saplings staked against the wind.
Blond sandstone blocks. Paths and steps that describe
the old shoreline. Darling Harbour below
the legs of skyscrapers, terraces, flights
of steps to the lawn, the centre of the headland
and all the footways leading down to water.

Fifty years ago I first came here,
walking north along Hickson Road and saw
the distant funnel, a passenger ship,
above the wharf sheds. I searched and found her,
Tjiluwah, only nine thousand tons, but a liner
and to me magical. I watched entranced.

Two hundred and sixty passengers, less
than a modern Airbus, sailing in luxury
north to Djakarta, Manila, Hong Kong.
I went on board and hovered in the buzzing crowd.
Today there are rocks where the wharf had been
and paths where the wharf sheds stood.

And *Tjiluwah* was sold, scrapped years ago,
a victim of early jumbos and jets.
I watch the harbour, blue as summer,
wrap myself in a coat against the wind,
cold, southerly. I compare then with now.
The park will be lovely when the trees grow.

An Old Mohawk

The New York Central Railroad was the only railway in the world to call their 4-8-2 mountain locomotives Mohawks, as there were no mountains on the NYC network.

September 1955,
somewhere west of Cleveland
a New York Central Mohawk
easing to a halt under the coal chute.

Express passenger locomotive
for top link streamliners
hauled at speed on the Water Level Route,
the Hudson River, New York
to Albany, on to Buffalo, Chicago.
Every inch a passenger engine,
her drop-coupler pilot, disc drivers,
twin smoke deflectors,
her smooth contours, feminine curves,
grace and speed, an aristocrat
of multiple-track mainlines,
varnish and sleeping cars, a lady
of the overnight expresses.

Fallen now on evil times –
displaced by diesels, the end of her life,
dirty, black, cylinder and steam dome covers
gone, booster engine removed
for ease of maintenance, today
hauling dead freight, anything she could pull –
a huge tonnage of empties, gondolas
of scrap iron, junk, bad-order cars
patched up for workshops or the cutting-torch,
end of days, just an extra, pick-up freight,
no priority, wait for anything else
anywhere on the track.

The engineer leans out, waiting.
He looked the part – alert and brawny,
goggles and cap, rakish moustache, all suggest
he'd a flair to make the cinders fly,
the quiet authority to run his engine,
in command, his train, no matter how lowly.
'A hundred cars? What speed d'ya expect
to make down the track?'
'60 miles an hour – oh, yes, we'll roll
once we get outa here,' he said.
An old Mohawk making a mile a minute
with a dead freight? I thought but didn't say,
that's optimism, rubbish, dismissed
the idea, walked away.

Hours later, 12 miles closer to Cleveland,
a track closed, signal failures, confusion,
passenger trains delayed, the Mohawk's extra
supposed to be stabled somewhere,
sidetracked out of the way, so the diesel varnish
could pass, but where? Where was she?
Miles back, delayed, broken down? But where?

A faint smudge of smoke on the horizon,
a distant whistling, a train, moving fast,
an express passenger, steam hauled, but which one?
Where on the timetable an express now?
Nothing now…a blast of exhaust, rolling like fate
down like the Day of Judgement, steam exhaust
cracking clear and sharp, valve gear notched up to centre
for the speed, alligator crossheads blurred,
main and side rods whirling, old NYC
heavy motion at speed, the crew relaxed,
enjoying the breeze, every revolution,
4 pairs, 69-inch drivers wheeling her train,
100 cars, rattling, reeling, rocking
nothing like the Twentieth Century Limited,
but driving on to Cleveland,
a mile a minute made with ease, gaining
momentum, accelerating, sheer guts
and determination, riding into
the distance at more than sixty,
just as her driver said she would.

The Energy of Spring

Thin clouds,
a washed-out hungry blue
like a bland backdrop
as the heat pours down.

The buildings sun their backs
to red and ochre, the tiles
and brickwork baked to blonde.
Trees chatter in the wind.

Self-controlled but vibrant,
the energy of spring
drives the day to loss and lust,
to starburst or to love.

Spring

after *May* by Uros Zupan

I saw it shimmering in the August winds.
When the year paused it stepped from the bush
slid into my room and announced itself
in the ancient language of trees,
in the voice of rain raising temples of water
onto the shoulders of air,
in the dreaming of owls and crabs
and in the first steps of young horses.

Then I felt the rain breathing and the rind
of the earth grow warm and rise like dough.
Now the warming rain rinses my windows
and the facades of houses across the street,
caresses the rough bark of gum trees,
and softens the cold faces of gravestones.

The morning awakes seraphim, conjures
the street into life and excites young girls
in their swinging skirts, their thighs alive
in their fragrant skin and their eyes like deer,
in brilliant smiles that echo and hover
into the evening when the cut grass weeps
with the soft, damp odour of the late sun
and the night buzzes with the cries of crickets
that melt into darkness like chocolate.

It's then that old Li Po, far into his wanderings
in the south and the west, visits me in moonshine
and kisses my brow with all the ease of the earth's
spontaneity, its presence, power and change.

Ordeal

I promise I'll make you sicker than you've ever been.
I'll claw my way into the bottom of your lungs
and screw stilettos of ice into every fibre of air
you manage to snatch,
torture you into coughing for weeks
so your nose and throat are raw
and you're drowning in the thick scum of yourself,
that food is impossible to eat,
to keep down or even think about
and you're retching in the bathroom and your head is clammy
with sweat and your eyes stick to their lids
and will not open.

But worse, I'll force you to ring the person
you're looking forward to meeting for afternoon tea
and cancel, because you're too sick to even leave your bed,
so that eight weeks later you still don't know
if you'll ever see each other again.

Nothing Like My life

Of course the pain
comes at night,
claw-clutch in the dark
flatworm hours
between night and nightmare,
the body's weak fulcrum,
the mind vulnerable
in the brittle skull
of thump and bedstead-twisting,
knock and writhing sleep.

The ambulance meanders
through red-dwarf streets,
traffic lights and shopfronts
of faint glass,
filtered into splinters,
punctured spasms
in the twilight flesh.

'Breathe into this…'

The world swings downward
through spirals of hypodermics,
narcotics of empty soft-world
and the dark comes again…

…another anaemic morning whines
to exhausted, dim, new light.

Confused by morphine,
the after-effects of pain,
half-asleep and half in vertigo,
somewhere in a cab
I cannot understand
why I'm taken home to bed
alone, strangely
floating in the morning
that's nothing like a dream
and nothing like my life.

Fromelles

A row of trees behind a flat,
ordinary field where something was buried once.
The long shadows of evening
and the shadows of the past.
Soldiers with bayonets at dawn, running
across the field but they don't run far.
Machine guns and mud
and the clay of the Somme
that hides and buries and preserves.

Billy Jones, David Smith, Robby White,
Johnny Brown and…and…
four pits, two where they are laid out
in neat military rows
and two where they are not,
a jigsaw of rotting uniforms and boots
and shards of bone and human flesh.

Prime ministers smile and shake the hands
of soldiers marching off to wars
in the sun, in public street parades,
on television and in news reports.
But here there are no photographs
or public access to the site,
only plastic screens to hide what's left of
Billy Jones, David Smith and Robby White,
Johnny Brown and…and…buried in the clay,
after the machine guns and the mud.

A War Memorial

A list of names
no one ever reads.
The children play in the park.
Their mothers stroll by
and the flowers look lovely
in the spring.
The inscription says
'Lest we Forget'
but we do forget
these men and women
from two world wars
and we have forgotten
the dead
from every other war
since then
and the names are just names
and the memorials are always stone.

The prime minister
stands and shakes the hands
of Australian soldiers
leaving for overseas
to fight someone
they've never heard of.
He gives every one of them
his best wishes
and looks serious for the camera.

But when they return
shattered
they can't get
psychological counselling
because we have new lists now
and the names are still just names
and the government
just can't afford it.

Ghosts and Dreams

from phrases by Marilynne Robinson in 'Lila'

The cinema's alive with ghosts and dreams.
Ghosts on the screen and ghosts who only watch
unreachable worlds where people's lives
are cared about even by strangers.
There are ghosts that float in huge, magnetic scenes
and ghosts that dream a stranger's dream, gathered
in the dark, all dreaming the same dream,
larger than they are, more significant, braver,

dreams so rich they shower our lives
with all the love we've always hungered for,
instil what's missing into all we have,
complete the incomplete, then swell beyond mere dreaming
to worlds so perfect they leave the dreamer stranded
looking inward like a stranger, like a ghost.

Opening Night

Of course, I'd give a lot to be
a groundling in Shakespeare's Old Globe Theatre,
to stand and gawp the opening night
of *Hamlet*, *Twelfth Night* or *King Lear*.

But given that, how could I know
the strange new show would be a hit?
I'd not suspect that in a hundred years
they'd say its Shakespeare's masterpiece.

A minor claim to fame I know and yet
I was a boy about fourteen,
a languid student after school,
a lazy, humid afternoon

and idly watched on Channel Two
a weird new show that came from Britain.
A boy and girl were walking home
surprised to see, archaic even then,

an old police box in a field.
Suspicious, curious and brave,
they're tricked and locked inside, kidnapped
away to awful other times and places.

A vicious, frightening old man,
evil, somehow other-worldly,
took them, held them in his will
and scared the living daylights out of me.

It wasn't *Hamlet* that I'd seen
but looking back I'm free to brag,
the Tardis, Time Lord, the very first,
in black-and-white and cheaply made…

I'm fifty-nine, at 8 o'clock
on Tuesday nights, my wife and I
just settle down and watch – vivid
coloured, expensive, smoothly made –

I can't keep count of forty years, yes more,
but two, three thousand episodes and on –
the longest running, most successful
TV series ever made, I think,

compelling, frightening, the opening night
of *Lear*, well, no – the low-key premiere
from Gallifrey, the chap with two hearts – yes,
episode one of *Doctor Who*.

6 a.m. Fog, Sydney, Early Winter

Walk out my door, the fog's like a trenchcoat.
Dark skeins, damp pleats and my collar's buttoned
under scarfs of mist. Lightshafts! I freeze!
Columns of headlights swirl and smoke in the gloom,
Dazzled in the yellow murk, the glare
focussed through a haze of lights, parallels
in sinister, machine guns and spies,
secret police. In the driveway
a waiting taxi, it's engine running…

Assess the situation – to my left
trees and the fence, right's the building,
a tenement back-alley, garages,
the driveway's cold searchlights and their target.
I've got to bluff, casual as I can,
adjust the brim of my grey fedora,
raise my collar, walk the sightlines, play brave,
don't run, don't look the victim, just walk,
breathe, keep breathing…

It's 1963, Checkpoint Charlie,
I'm leaving The Zone – this spy
stays out in the cold. It's Volksprater,
Vienna, 1946 and I'm Harry Lime.
It's Cold War London, George Smiley
walks le-Carre-land and that's the KGB.

Midnight soon, the *hauptbahnhof,* Frankfurt?
1939, no Star of David
on my sleeve, a fake passport aches in my pocket
and the last sleeping-car express
in seven minutes to the Swiss border.
The locomotives steam and smoke, injectors
stamp and hiss. Lightshafts! I freeze! Parked there
in the driveway, engine running,
the big, black, Gestapo limousine,
the last express…headlights…

I'm Humphrey Bogart and my girl
is Ingrid Bergman. This is my story.
That right, schweetheart?

On the Death of Slobodan Milosevic

Time brings the death even of monsters.

A massive heart attack at 64,
the fourth year of trial
for Crimes Against Humanity…

A bullet to the head
in a concrete bunker
deep below Potsdammer Platz
in the ruins of the Reich…

At the end of a rope in Spandau Prison…

Torn to pieces in the street…

Insane the desire
to reconstruct the future
on a foundation of bones.

History's written by the strong.
Relaxed and comfortable
dictators pass away of age
in Beijing, Madrid and Santiago
or a village in Cambodia.

And those who win their wars of bones
embalmed like dolls,
may lie in state for years,
revered like Uncle Jo
whose soldiers won the Great and Patriotic War
and then the Gulags…

Monsters of a new century
already lust to redesign the lives
of babies not yet born,
lie in interviews on TV
and are very good at euphemism –

ethnic cleansing
and the Pacific Solution,

Mandatory Detention
and Year Zero,

the Final Solution,
a War on Terror

The Father of Ashes

The sky blazes
and the wind coils in the stars
like a dream of the future

but there is no narrative of light.
The eyes of our lovers
do not burn in the sky.

The dark passage of a storm
hides the chimera of constellations
and shakes the ribs of the earth

where we stand
among the bone-thin trees.
In the wind there is no message

we can decipher
and the stars burn themselves
to ashes anyway.

Berry Mountain Road

The autumn we strolled
the Unter den Linden,
Alexander Platz to the Brandenburg Gate,
the wind collected avenues of leaves.

The paths through the Tiergarten
were damp beneath our boots
and crisp with brown and red.
A skyline of cranes and reconstruction.

A narrow, winding road
from the high ridges in the sky,
rolls down Berry Mountain to the coast,
blue with the sun and green in the valleys.

A skyline carved with rocks and blue-gums.
The autumn we strolled
the Unter den Linden, we also rode
that high and ancient highway home.

'Home'

Never became Australian.
Migrated after World War One,
the General Strike, Depression,
no home there fit for heroes.
'Home' for my grandparents
fifty years later
was still the rural outskirts
of Derby, Australia
just the suburbs
of provincial minds,
a place they just
happened to be.

For a small boy 'home'
was neatly sliced in two
by ambiguities of post-war
distance, Berlin's Iron Curtain,
Germanies and Koreas of Cold-War
childhood, never exactly here,
not definitely somewhere else
but strange amalgams
of English and Australianess,
place names not so far
from the windward side of anywhere.
Our trips to town passed
Croydon, Lewisham, Petersham
or by ferry berthed at Greenwich.
The ABC News always followed
'And at home…' with stories
of foreign and outlandish places –
Kings Cross, Liverpool, Melbourne.

Knowledge of Sydney
overlaid the ghostly streets of London.
Learned quickly, could
find my childish way
anywhere – when Dad said
we'd walk to Hyde Park
I was sorry not to see the queen.
As any nong should know
Buckingham Palace stood close by
Hyde Park Corner and the Queen
ruled Australia easily
from there.

Twenty years later
wrapped and scarfed against
an English winter, soft rain
brushed against my cheek.
Strode down the Mall
towards the great grey palace,
squat against an English sky,
no Sydney Sandstone here,
no streets of romance
grasped in half-forgotten tales
of 1920s Midland towns.
I thought whatever this to me
it isn't 'home'.

Names can conjure
all the wonders of the world,
Surabaya, Zamboanga, Esfahan.
I've learned home's
no place to pin a life to,
but all the places
equally one's own –
home is just yourself
at peace,
alone.

Finger Wharf

Nave and aisles hewn with hardwood,
arcades of columns parallel
the length of the pier, branched upward
into metal arches like muscles
clenched to the timber roof, a clerestory
of windows high on the walls
The gape of doorways which once slid
wide to the wharf, cargoes hoisted
in slings from the holds of freighters
into here, these warehouse vastnesses.

The finger wharf (Walsh Bay 2 and 3)
from the early twentieth century's
commercial hand, the industrial arm
and shoulder of the old port.
Winches, derricks, the cargo nets,
trucks and wharfies, the crunch and clang
from ships unloaded here, liners
hauled with hawsers, taut on bollards,
their bows raised high on Hickson Road.
This storehouse built for everything
that came by sea – all then came by sea,
now has chairs and lounges for the comfort
of visitor and audience.

Cathedral of form and function, theatre
of height and length, the spaciousness of talk,
performance, lectures and ideas.
The ships, the cargoes that passed through here,
have left nothing, only the space itself,
and ghosts rusted into poetry,
the huge constructions of the living past.

Reservoir Street, Surry Hills

The street sweeps up the hidden escarpment,
lifts away from the railway viaduct,
a sandstone dog sprawled across its feet,
turns its back on Elizabeth Street
between the buildings officiously plump
on the corner and apartment blocks,
mustered like a guard of honour, aloof
observant as sergeants, unreadable and cool,
behind the windows, shops and furniture, foyers
and cafes, their tables spilled along the street,
whose patrons chat and drink like calm civilians
while armies gather and the seasons change.

The street moves up the hidden escarpment,
between laneways narrow as eyes
and terrace houses stacked shoulder to shoulder
like drinkers in dishevelled bars
that fit the corner like a brown akubra.
The occasional spiv, neat and quiet
in a blue suit – a newly painted door
that opens to display another small,
unfashionable room, quaintly furnished,
that might be safe but might bewilder you.
The Chinese laundry steams on the comer.

The street claws up the hidden escarpment,
a canyon camouflaged by cliffs of brick,
of clean mosaics, steel and girders, new
facades flashing in the sun and the frames
of branches, winter plane trees motionless
against a chequerboard of high verandas,
starting backwards into privacy and shade.

The street curves up the hidden escarpment,
away from the gentry, new centuries of trend
and fashion, into remnants of older squalor,
mid-Victorian, built for workers, decayed paint,
derelict and tenements, houses fit for dolls,
rotting balconies, step by step the march
of tiny terraces and railings up the street
and capped teeth, warehouse buildings, earlier decades
the last slum-clearance century, abandoned
and forlorn among the latte-led economies
of size and waste and onto Riley Street
where workmen renovate the Royal Hotel
and the old reservoir lies hidden behind bricks.

Now

It is always now.
Write your poems of burning blue
and the faintest of lines
becomes sharper
than your clearest memory.

There is no highway
into the past
and the future dies in the sun.

Coming is an empty promise
and departure leaves no trace.

'It is always now',
the poet writes
and the prophet
knows this too.

The Horse and the Cattle Dog

Profoundly deaf,
our old, red cattle dog
mooching around,
quietly scavenging
in the neighbour's paddock.

A young horse,
playful, just loved
to stampede
the Jack Russell puppies
into flocks of flying white.

A galloping juggernaut
of flashing hooves
careering down
directly from behind
suddenly a cartoon coyote
bought to a screeching,
road-runner stop.

Ever seen a horse stunned,
dismayed?
'That didn't work – what the hell
to do now?'

We yelled,
'Mindy, watch out!'
Galvanised with shock,
old Mindy was a red streak
under our fence.

Tables turned,
the safer side of barbed wire,
she hurled
volleys of abuse,
sustained barrages of fire,
whole broadsides
of armour-piercing,
high-explosive
barking:
'Ya rotten nag!
Think ya can scare me?
Horse meat!
Sneak up, will ya!
Dead meat!
Paddy nag!
Horse creap!'

The nag wandering away,
crestfallen.
Mindy was still the boss

Toby

Hard to believe
our neighbour's playful
and affectionate Jack Russell,
energetic, mischievous,
little Toby,
tug-a-tobes, chase-a-ball,
race-around-madly dog,
ride-in-the-car,
wrestle-and-cuddle-you dog,
dig holes, roll-on-the-grass dog,
passionate tummy tickle,
asleep on the armchair,
small, around-the-house dog

is the direct descendent
of Siberian wolves.

The predator's eyes
beyond the shadow light,
haunter of campfire dreams,
northern ice-dark fog and forest –
they still lurk in the cries
of small children.

Indistinct the packs prowl
on the furthest edge
of here
and almost everywhere.

On Mount Athos the gates
of medieval monasteries
at sundown
are still locked
against the coming
of the wolves

and liturgies
for daughters of the light
chant
against the she wolves'
howling night.

We still fear the small races –
imps and gnomes.
On Flores
their bones exist.
The Neanderthals
we hope
are still extinct.

Late Afternoon, Camperdown Park

Walking back to the car,
turned the corner
of St Stephen's Cemetery
and the green vista opened up
of the park:

groups of people sitting, lying
on the grass chatting,
lovers in pairs,
dogs chasing balls
and exploring, playing, sniffing
as dogs do,
boys kicking a football, as boys do,
a group of jugglers practising
and a high-wire walker,
his wire strung between two trees.

Seven on a summer's evening
and a soft nor'easter blowing,
the humidity of the day
replaced by cool,
the world relaxed, at play.

From the trees,
behind the churchyard walls,
the stonework needle
of St Stephen's spire.
Over there rows of local houses
and the rest of the world
in the far distance, fading away,
nowhere near here…

A Mad Moon

The evening traffic and the heat
The smell of car exhaust
and gasoline
cling to the humid air.

A mad moon boils in a black
and threatening sky.
Thunderclouds on a jagged
horizon.

Commuters read
the evening papers
headlines again of war
and financial collapse.

A man walks two small dogs.

They strain against the leash.

It

They stood and watched it in the dark.
The wind was rising in the south
and all the waves pursued
their purpose and their breath.

It broke like caverns under stars
It came and burst like thunder,
passed like music over sand.
They stood and pondered, strained to mark

its movement through their night.
Bright eyes searched its meaning
in the rhythms of their lives
and in the circles of the stars.

On the Hawkesbury

A deserted upper deck,
light rain sweeps downriver
and the sky is grey,
a cold wind blowing.

The river is grey, the clouds grey
and headlands slide into the rhythm
of the river and its far reaches,
flows of water from the earth
fathoms deep,
and the unremitting bush,
a wilderness of green
and the distant cliffs,
walls of sandstone…

My jacket is wrapped close,
my cap and my face damp.
I stare into the rain upriver
seeing for the first time
reach upon reach,
the great, grey waterway twining inland
like the lifeblood
of a new continent,
like an explorer of a new world…
realise for the first time in years,
there is not one sign
of the civilised world,
not one man-made object anywhere,
only the bush and the river
and the rain
spreading out like a blueprint
of the human heart.

A River, Anywhere

Not the dreamer nor the dreamed
at the edge of dreams
walks the winding road

beyond the midnight ferry
or takes to the hills
above the dark river.

Here is a sign,
a jetty
and a gate.

Travellers huddle
into passports and they question
the ferryman

who is helpful and smiles
as black water
laps through the valleys.

Behind the morning,
bridges burn as if
deep water never flows.

Here, half-empty bottles of pain.
The road winds to the hills
where no one ever goes.

Old Paris

A photo by Eugene Atget

Below an archway
of the old, stone bridge,
two stub-nosed barges
tethered to the quay
and every flagstone sharp,
exact.

The black-nosed barges
and the quayside, curve away
and everything
is grey and distance –
the river's mist and fog,
cold, deserted, ghostlike.

Sullivan's Cove, Midnight

The crowds have drifted out
of Salamanca Place, trawlers
rock and rhythm to the swells
in Constitution Dock.
Orchestras and choirs
bob to a tune of tides.
Traffic and batons of light
focus on the harbour.
Spotlights hum
on cranes and wharves.

Rockets of gulls
flow and hover on the bridge,
a slow march of columns,
slim shivers of wind.
Lights from the city spill
across neat, dry streets
and confident in red and green
rows of navigation buoys
to all the inland reaches sing.

A black river
beats beneath the lamps,
laps the foot of piers.
Wide winds bite,
ferry themselves downstream.
Highways roll in the night.
Huge channels
widen to a waste of waves,
drum and moan to the bay of storms,
the Great Southern Ocean,
the endless continent of ice.

Tides that sweep
through the morning
are silent and black as they turn.
Only the swirling of night,
immense its ebb to the sea,
sings in the rivers of ice.

No New Start

My desk lamp glows precise and sharp tonight.
A fresh nor'easter scours the room.
My window opens onto cool and calm
after the day's sweat. It seems to lift a weight,
the brute, humid oppression and the heat.
Today a new president's been sworn
to office, a new breathing for the world.
The tenth my lifetime – all were fresh to start.

To a troubled student – 'Don't flee, Irene.'
There's always demons at your head. The same old curse,
now and here and yours. Fight them, babe. Stay sane.
Another window – yellow excavators cruise
like ancient reptiles across the building site.
Mr President. Irene. The old demons. Of course.

White

It's a white world.
The wind snatches gum leaves
and hurls them sideways,
twists the undersides
of branches towards the sun,
a torrent of leaves
like bodies too long shaded
by winter, now
exposed and gibbering,
victims of the white wind,
floating in air,
falling on crushed grass,
like snowflakes and ghosts.

The Mist

If you walk out
into the mist,
it retreats
just beyond
your arms' reach,
like a white narrative
of joy, like a vision
of the future
but your woollen coat
catches the moisture
and is damp
so you've merged into the mist
which is also behind you
and is your past.

Widow

Beneath the moon there is a hill
whose slopes rise towards it.
Beneath the hill there is a church
whose tower reaches towards it.
In the churchyard there is a gravestone
bathed in moonlight

and a dark woman who stands beside it,
who gazes at the moon
and raises her arms towards it
and doesn't stop crying.

Untitled

after a photograph by Christian Blanchard

Push, push against the pane.
You're trapped behind the glass.
The factory view, suburban noir.

Black, black the colour of your dress,
your gloves, the horizontal bars,
parallels and slats that guard

the floor-length windows, the glass
you press against your palms. The view
outside is white, a white obsession with air

and the whiteness of the sun
that isn't here. The mist, limitations
of morning and you behind the glass,

heels raised with the effort,
your head turned, longing for the embrace
of what and where. You, untitled,

unlisted here. There, a string of pearls,
beaded down your back, your skirt
swollen like a parachute, your hair

swept up and you're invited, dressed
made up for the thin formalities
of windows that keep you here.

The Cathedral

To sit in the dormer window,
this small hotel in Regensburg.
An ambience of solid calm
in a white and spartan, silent room.
The view embraces roofs and spires.
A medieval, summer's night
settles gently on cathedral lights,
centuries softened in this ancient town.

The floodlit pile of mellow walls
and arches, pinnacles and towers,
the flying-buttressed, gothic sails
invoke a fantasy, a ship
of creed and faith, a jewelled ark
of prayers and air, of awe and stone.

UTS Tower, Broadway

Concrete set in narrow bands,
window slits like shuffled cards,
blocks roughened slab on slab,
laid and layered, a stack
of horizontals
stair-cased into forty storeys
that echo earthen tones
and strata.

A Mayan massif
multiplied in steps.

A single digit – unity
added, repeated, multiplied
and piled heavy-handed
onto the floating sky,
that lacks every quality of air
except for height and size.

Central Park, Broadway

Red the lights of the traffic moving uphill.
White headlights sliding towards us,
the street, the red and green of traffic lights
and the neon of restaurants and shops.

Pedestrians, single and in groups,
men in suits going home, youngsters on the town
and the people getting onto buses
and others stepping down as we breathe
together hand in hand through the crowds,
up Broadway, Thursday night, uphill towards
Railway Square, the steps going down,
the tunnel to the trains and us walking close,
our shoulders brushing…

This is normal, this is real and yet
over there, a monolith – that building
huge in its change of scale, like a machine
glowing, a black screen that covers half the sky,
pulses of red and illuminations
above us, blotting out the street below,
holding out an arm towards us, as if
a whole new planet there, or a finger
of a god that signs, 'Now, thou shalt'
or 'Now thou shalt not'. Read! Obey!

Reflections

Reflections boil like mist
away from the mirror's surface,
the tidal trough, the dying day.
Sliding through the interface a train.

It winds past the window
like a hot river, the fierce sun
mellows into clouds, fairy rain
and multicoloured blocks, steel

containers bright with ambient light.
From the depths of the mirror's face
come the red-river tides
alive in your flashing eyes.

New Tickets

There's a yellow moon tonight,
yesterday a yellow sun.
I do not feel a difference.
There's nowhere left to run.

I do not see the cockroach
scuttling in the dark.
I will not be an insect
hiding in the murk.

I will not submit to terror
under a yellow moon.
I will not be the victim
of an alien sun.

I stand at the kitchen window.
I search the depths of the cupboard.
I open up the drawer
and reach for a yellow knife.

At night I check my emails.
The darkness in the cupboard
brings darkness to the screen.
Where will I stand tomorrow?

I see the scuttling cockroach.
I cannot see my hand.
I see the yellow darkness
smothering the land.

There are aphids on the roses,
blight on the other plants,
swine flu rides the atmosphere.
There's a darkness surrounding you.

You sneeze and turn away from me

and looking in your bag,
below the keys and wallet,
a knife and two new tickets,
the tickets are yellow too.

Perfection

We all dream
of writing the perfect poem,
to capture all creation
in a line.

We all dream
of being loved
unreservedly
for ourselves alone.

Where is the perfect poem?
Rarely, I feel the muse
stirring dimly
deep within my bones.

And where the perfect lover?
Ah! For that
we must ask the child
and its mother.

J.M.W. Turner: *The Fighting Temeraire*, 1838

A sun of blood
and yellow
streams across the sea.
Reflections in black.
A steam tug
belches smoke.
Ghosts from a past
bleached like corpses
in the mist
and a white procession
of wooden ships
curves to infinity.

The old ship's
a bone,
the shipbreaker's
boneyard.
The seas were hot
with corpses
at Trafalgar, Cape St Vincent
and the Nile.

Temeraire's
tugged landwards
like a whale.
A thousand tars
killed in broadsides
and by shot
rolled in foam
on Spanish beaches
and red sunsets
blanched them white
as old ships
waterlogged by time
in backwaters and the same
unclean tides.

In the desert
B52s in lines
wait for the scrapper's torch,
but they're black
and the sky's
already bloody.

Irene, Dance

Parallel scars on your upper arms
like the gate to a garden of smiles
or bars on the entrance to love.
The tiger that rides your shoulder,

a kanji whose words are a song.
A song whose words are a dance.
Your badge is the heart you wear
on your sleeve – the snarl and the claw

and the blister. Your stripes, your voice,
the old guilt, the old pain. Ditch them, babe!
Be the tiger. Be the lover.
Smile. Sing the words, Irene. Dance.

Black Curtains

for Tonie, killed in a car accident, 1987

In the lonely hours
of early morning,
when the door quietly opens
and a girl
walks through the room
and turns off the lamp,
you're still here
like a wolf note
in a string,
the black curtains moving
though the window's closed,
the unused candles.

I've never felt your ghost
but there is a presence here
and why should I
mention you tonight,
in this small back-room
I've shared for one hectic hour.
Just conversation
or are you
still significant
after twenty years?

I met you only once
though you were the first,
then all the others followed.

The Well

after Sofia Parnik

Workers are cutting a hole
into the brilliant blue of the ice.

Is it a shaft for fish to breathe
or access for the lines of fishermen?

Is it a well for villagers
who'll trudge with buckets of fresh water

or an escape hatch for an exhausted wayfarer
who's found that she and her life

are travelling on different highways
and she has nowhere else to go?

Back Veranda

A veranda the length of the house.
a loggia or the aisle of a cathedral.
The bricks, sills and windows of the back wall.
Opposite, eight timber, brown-clad columns,
precise, at intervals, like monks at prayer,
who've arranged themselves in procession
before an arcade of shrubs lined like penitents.
Behind are the larger trees and their shade
over the shadowed lawn, sloping down
from enclosed space, high windows dim with light.

Tranquil, contained, domestic, the veranda
white-roofed and precise, is lined with pot-plants,
metal chairs and tables, other chairs of plastic,
and the long avenue of patterned tiles,
red sienna, like a pathway into foliage
and rays of the sun trespassing through trees,
an invasion of heat into cloisters of cool,
that highlights rows of washing hung to dry
as if the world intrudes with loud, rock music
into plainsong, chant and the privacy of prayer.

It's a Right

In the USA
a five year old boy,
while playing
with his grandfather's gun
shot and killed his baby brother.

Now Australians would say
that's the reason
guns should be banned,
no one should have them,

but I'm American and I know better
I'm a Christian, Republican, gun-club
shooter and member of the NRA,

so I know this is certainly true:
nine month old babies
should all have guns
to protect themselves
from their older brothers.

Sonnet 127 Again

Coal-black has rarely been considered fair
or if so, no one says its beautiful
but now I'm saying black is beauty's heir
as fair is now false and artificial,
since Photoshop makes the natural false,
fairing the foul with fake and cheaply young
and beauty's made with airbrush, make-up, else
by surgery and dark's been rinsed to blonde.
Therefore my lover's eyes are raven black,
her eyebrows dark as Spanish widows seem
to women not born fair, who never lack
cosmetic beauty's tricks at self-esteem.
Yet black clothes borrow sable from her hair
and in her eyes fashion knows beauty's there.

Sharrukina Reads 'The Outcast'

You read my poem thoughtfully, then fired
a grave and forthright, so unexpected response.
Incisive, certainty in every word and phrase,
to probe forensically your own character and soul.

Dominant, energetic, strong – a hint
of something softer and more delicate,
so vulnerable below the brash and self-assured.
I'd never thought of you at any time,

in any way, an outcast – far too confident,
although minority of culture, language, race,
your birthplace, and teenage immigrant as well,
gave every sign of standing angled to the group.

You keep your real self private, deep, so safe
from all sticky-fingered probing by the obtuse,
insensitive and crude, too precious
and too fine for this rough world to haggle over

and despoil. I see that clearly now and more.
I'm flattered to be trusted, thought worthwhile enough,
your heart to stand there naked. I'm proud my poem
evoked this honesty, such beauty and such truth.

After the Explosion

There is silence
and the silence lingers
and the silence is profound.

After the blast
there is nothing
and the nothing is widespread
and shocking.

After the explosion
there is smoke
and the smoke is stifling
and everywhere.

Then there is moaning.
Then there are screams
and the wail of ambulances.

There are bodies in the street
and blood on the ground
after the bomb.

Just Stepping Out

Every poem's a sprint
into the wind's howl,
the blizzard of ice-shriek,
Antarctica's word-flow.

Sheet-stressed syllables
and storm-stones of vowels,
white-overs and sense-blind,
crevasses of fail.

Step into the page-storm,
its frostways and pen streaks,
the hollows of snowfall,
a compass of half-rhyme.

My pen is my ice pick.
'I may be some time.'

At Night

Moon-lovers naked
in the frank stare
of the ogling sun –
birthmarks, scars, wrinkles, flab –
feel responsible
starkly for themselves,
judged by those they do not know
and cannot trust.

But dressed in the uniform
of night,
secure and safe
in a blur of boundaries,
confusion of limits,
they expand to abstractions,
transcend even themselves
and melt comfortably
into greatcoats of black
that soften the sharp world
with opportunities
and power.

From the Bistro

Inside the glass looking out,
the movement of feet in the arcade,
sip your coffee, order a meal…

and there outside the wall
the spectral walkers hold your gaze,
hurrying to the station, glancing
at the shops, going home or just
drifting like ghosts:

the girl carrying flowers,
men identical in suits, women
like wraiths in heels, the thin man
shimmers in a T-shirt, holds a jacket,
schoolgirls in dark, blue uniforms
like policemen…all pass,

capture your gaze but only for seconds,
so quickly gone, and the phantom stream
flows in the glass, your coffee cold,
meal uneaten yet, all pass,
all are gone, so quickly, just a metre
away, less, on the other side
of the glass – reach out, raise your hand,

the see-through barrier
you cannot penetrate or shatter,
between the living and…

The Pain From the Past is Always Present

The pain from the past is always present,
traces of memory, the nerve connections.
You think you're at peace but you never are –
the latest events spark old reactions.

Traces of memory, the nerve connections
charge up the impulse to protect your rights.
The latest events spark old reactions
to crush this new threat before it happens.

Charge up the impulse to protect your rights –
attack if you must and attack him first
to crush this new threat before it happens.
You're fighting the battles from years ago.

Attack if you must and attack him first –
don't accept the defeats you suffered once –
you're fighting the battles from years ago
and this time you're strong so this time you win.

Don't accept the defeats you suffered once.
Experience swells to a weapon now
and this time you're strong so this time you win.
The pain from the past is always present.

Smile

The night entices
my eyes
with the cold, hard light
of stars.

The moon brushes
my cheek
with warm fingers,
beams and shadows.

The wind tosses
my hair
in ruffles and impulses
of disarray

while your arms
are intertwined with mine
and your smile
illuminates the sky.

Potential

After humidity and heat,
arid skies bullied by the sun,
comes April lost in mist.

Jagged parapets, the cliffs and hills
gather into clouds of grey, enshroud
the valley, silks swathed in white

and the ambiguity of showers
like the fat sky breathing, the trees
swollen fur balls of leaves.

The air's no longer thick with steam
but brisk with the tongue of autumn,
licks your skin with cool clarity

as the season edges towards the cold,
the precursor of winter, the year's
potential teetering on the cliffs of change.

Birdsong

The screech of a satin bower bird
above the hiss of the rain,
unearthly, like the music of the moon
floating above the hills.

Then rolling thunder, an overture
to darkness and dampness and this closing in
of evening, the air furry with moisture,
the leaves all pointing to the rain

as if the fragility of the moon
is the singer's voice, birdsong
and rain the lyrics of a hymn
and a melody sinuous as the night.

Thunderclouds

An urban sunset.
Red roofs of tiles
and the grey skirts of clouds
reflect the sun.

The rain quickly transits
on its path to the sea.
Clouds brush past
returning.

The thin new path
hugs the curves
of the ancient river.
It winds through parks and trees.

Children grasp
their mothers' hands.

Just as the shadows lengthen
black cockatoos roost
in the high trees.
They shriek to each other
and shower passersby
with sticks and leaves.

Thunderclouds build
above the treetops.

Thunderstorm

Thunder rolls in from the hills,
rumbles as the world clears its throat,
the clash of bowling balls and sonic booms
chain-linked in jets, drums, shrapnel blasts,
seethings of the violent air.

This storm lurches and shudders,
an immense drunkard who stumbles
in a blind roar and fury, grinds
his fists against the hills, spits
jagged profanities of light,
and spittle rain in the sky's cold tantrum.

A giant baby hurls in temper
down in a black sulk that cracks
its cradle in the clouds, withdraws then
into a slow drizzle and mist
that muffles the shaken valley into
the turmoil of the sky's silence.

Vibrant

After rain
the landscape glows in a grey sky
with the green lustre
of what's fat and swollen.

Grey underscores the verdancy
of leaf and grass
as a dull canvass supports
the artist's gaudy paint.

A green almost beyond green,
thick and glowing
with the wet smell of soil
and moisture ringing

in significant air,
solid with damp
that before was vacant,
now vibrant, clean, clinging,

like the arms of a lover,
water dripping from leaves
like skin, soft
with the taste of rain.

Like Losing Skin

Eighteen months ago
you were frightened to meet me.
'What should I say to him?'
I did most of the talking.

You listened and assessed.

Yesterday, you were happy to meet
for tea and biscuits again.
I listened and you talked –
eighteen months later no need to assess.

We chatted, held hands, looked
into the other's eyes (yours are brown,
mine blue) like lovers
for two hours…more. Between us,

not a moment of silence.
Then I watched you walk away
through the arcade and when you waved
it was like losing skin.

Christmas 2014

This year is falling to its end,
time now for me to write the verse
that makes this new card I've chosen
personal, meaningful, true for you;
that makes my present something more
than just a gift – a thing unique
that no one else could give, no one
ever could, that you'll keep and prize

as yet another new year slides in
and we say this'll be the one,
only good will come, but really know
all will be very much the same
as the one that's gone, except, I hope,
for this small poem I wrote for you.

A Dress of Words

I'll write you a dress made of words
that shimmers in linen and rhyme
and sparkles with similes wrought with gold,
that swirls with the letters of alphabets
in stitches of verse and seams of vowels
that wrap on your thighs like a verb,
that'll stun with metaphors sewn with silk
in your glamour, your poise and your style.

I'll write you a gown made of lyrics
with the gracious lilt of ancient ballads,
that you'll wear in the moon and the starlight,
you'll wear in elegies written to soft,
the elegance of bards and their voices
in the flowing hems of angels' skirts.

Night Ferry to Abbotsford

for Robert Dickins

Nose into darkness – the river's passage
a pathway rolling between the lights
of suburbs, twisting through star clusters,
part of the sky, part of the earth,
soft as velvet beneath our keel.

Scent the channel, meander wharf to wharf,
shudder to a stop and wait – passengers
depart and we glide on, slide into black
as if this sudden oasis of light
is a small place, wharf and steps, nothing else,
beside a highway streaming into midnight,

as if the river is merely outskirts
of a well-lit world, not the bloodstream
of its life and our ferry a warm cell,
the bright corpuscle of a spark
that leaves oxygen burning in its wake.

The River and the City

At Parramatta it's a small, brown river
forced into itself, hemmed by mangroves
and the ferry crawls at seven knots
like a cautious crab, along the single track,
feeling for the channel, tied between the red
and green pylons like railway sleepers,
searching for depth, awkward and uncertain.

At Drummoyne the river's a broad, grey runway
that builds along new reaches and swells like a child
approaching adolescence, still hemmed by suburbs,
the latticework of wharves and houses.
Water slides below the great, curved arch
that strides across the sky encased in concrete.

The ferry slows past boat sheds and stone walls,
noses into bays, approaches the escarpment
at Darling Harbour, hesitant there
in the folds and foothills pushing into Pyrmont.

From the river, the city's a mountain range,
erupts vertically on the scale of giants,
built on platforms of rock, triple headlands,
rounded cliffs of sheer glass and peaks spiked
in steel, new columns, cordilleras
melting into plateaux and sierras
that jostle and melt the sky into faraway.
The abrupt stop at King Street Wharf. The wait.

Stealthy as a cat, bypass Barangaroo,
dodge the finger wharves that reach out at Walsh Bay,
embrace the Quay, snuggle home past *Diamond Princess*,
floating hotel, all horizontals and length,
ninety thousand tons, terraces and balconies,
the whole safe length of western Sydney Cove,
where the river meets the city
and the city meets the sky.